THE ULT WHOLEFOODS COOKBOOK

30 Days To A New You, Health, And Body

DIANA WATSON

Table of Contents

Introduction

Congratulations on purchasing your personal copy of *The Ultimate Whole Foods Cookbook.* Thank you so much for doing so!

The following chapters in this cookbook will cover the basics of what the Whole Diet is all about and how you can successfully incorporate it into your everyday lifestyle! While there are many other Whole Diet cookbooks on the market, this one covers the absolute basics that you will need to begin your trek down a healthier lane TODAY. This book also contains some of the best recipes from the World Wide Wed, incorporated with recipes that my family, friends and I have tried and enjoyed!

You will discover how important is it to be able to eat healthier on YOUR terms and how this ultimately leads to success in achieving your weight loss goals and assisting in leading a much healthier lifestyle, all while not having to sacrifice delicious tastes!

Eating in regards to the Whole Foods Diet is not about eating only certain ingredients like some of those other pesky diet fads, but rather eating less of the food groups that are not so good for our bodies. Our bodies are our temple, so why not fuel it with the best edibles that we can possibly consume? It is a no-brainer!

There are plenty of books on this the Whole Diet on the market, thanks again for choosing this one! Every effort was made to ensure it is full of as much useful information as possible. Please enjoy!

The Basics of the Whole Diet

Congratulations! If you are reading the first chapter of this book, that means you have decided to take a crucial step in creating a healthier life for yourself and that decision alone is no easy feat! This chapter is all about what the Whole diet is, along with what and what not to consume during the course of these vital 30 days. If you have decided to give this diet a try, then you need to be aware that you must be truly committed to wanting to make a change for yourself, as this diet will be asking you to dedicate your time and will-power to sticking directly to the rules of this program.

The Whole diet is quite the rage nowadays and it is likely that you have heard about it via social media or friends and family. It has also been commonly referred to as more of an "anti-diet" rather than a regular diet fad, for it is better described as a lifestyle change. The diet itself was designed to be a learning process that you could take along with you for the rest of your life after the initial 30 days. To be able to truly fuel your body in better ways, one must be knowledgeable of how certain edibles affect you. The Whole Diet is a perfect blend of the Paleo Diet along with the process of elimination that targets getting rid of foods that are responsible for inflammation within the body.

The Whole Diet takes crap from no one and says that there is no such thing as "slipping up" when it comes to cheating while on it. Once you know which foods to keep yourself from consuming, you must keep them out of your life as you retrain your body not to crave them. That is the entire goal of this 30-day diet: to identify the bad foods and 100% eliminate them from your diet for hopefully, well, forever. This means you must be prepared to make this type of lifestyle change, for it won't be the easiest thing to rid yourself of your everyday bowl of ice cream or other bad eating habits.

The good news? There are plenty of recipes out there that you can consume that are delicious enough to keep you from thinking about those edibles you crave every day. The best place to start is within the other chapters of this book when searching for recipes to incorporate into your life.

The Whole Day Rules

Do's

- **Consume real foods**

    o Eat foods such as eggs, seafood, and meat in moderated proportions.

    o Lots of vegetables

- Portioned fruits

- Lots of seasonings, spices, herbs, and natural fats

- Foods with fewer ingredients are far better. This means that they are more than likely less processed than foods with long ingredient lists.

- Look for foods that contain ingredients you can pronounce

- **Don'ts: To be avoided for 30 days**

- **No junk foods, baked good or other goodies with "approved" components**

  - Any of these types of edibles, even those

with ingredients that are "technically" within Whole limitations, disregard the entire point of going on this diet, to begin with. It will compromise your potential results.

- **No sulfites, MSG or carrageenan**
- **No dairy**

  - o Includes sheep, goat and cow milk
  - o Includes frozen yogurt, ice cream, sour cream, yogurt, kefir, cheese, cream, and milk

- **No legumes**

  - o Includes beans of ALL kinds
  - o Includes peanut butter and other such butters
  - o Includes soy in ALL forms

- **No grains**

  - o Includes:

    - Sprouted grains, sorghum, bulgur,

millet, rice, corn, oats, barley, rye, and wheat

- ALL gluten-free cereals: quinoa, buckwheat, etc
- Also includes processes in which the above are added into foods. ***Important to read food labels***.

- **No alcohol**
- **No sugar**

  o This includes both real and artificial kinds of sugar

- **Do not step on the scale or take measurements for entire 30 days**

    o This diet is not only about weight loss, but curbing your bad eating habits which will lead to benefits that have the potential to last a lifetime.

    o **Exceptions – Allowed during the course of the Whole Diet**

- **Salt**
- **Coconut aminos**
- **Vinegar**
- **Particular legumes**

- o Snow and sugar snap peas and green beans are allowed. These foods are pods rather than beans.

- **Fruit juices**
- **Clarified butter or ghee**
- **You have ONE job – Let Whole Diet Do the Rest**
- Your job while on the course of this diet is to stay away from food that is off limits and fulfill your stomach with the edibles that are allowed. There is no need for the hassle of constantly weighing yourself. These is no need to write down weekly measurements. There is no reason to count all those calories that you consume. There are no requirements to waste your hard earned money on buying organic

products. If you learn how to truly reside closely to the Whole rules for the entirety of 30 consecutive days, the diet will provide you with spectacular results! The remainder of this book is filled with delectable recipes to fulfill your cravings and keep you on the right track while on the Whole Diet.

-
-
-
-
-
-
-

Whole Breakfast Recipes

Zucchini Noodle Breakfast Bowl

What's in it:

- Salt and pepper
- 2 tbsp. green onion
- 2 eggs
- 2 sweet potatoes
- 1-2 cloves of garlic
- 2 tbsp. water
- ¼ c. olive oil
- ½ avocado
- 1-2 zucchinis

How it's made:

- Skin sweet potatoes and proceed to cut them into bite sized pieces. In a skillet, heat olive oil over medium heat and cook potatoes, ensuring to stir occasionally.
- Take zucchini, cut off ends and then put through a spiralizer and set to the side.
- Avocado cream: Put water, 2 tablespoons olive oil, garlic and avocado into food processor and pulse, adding more olive oil if needed
- Pour avocado cream over zucchini noodles and toss until coated. Take cooked and lightly browned potatoes and pour over noodles
- Utilizing the skillet you cooked potatoes in, cook your eggs until they are done to your liking and put over top of noodles.
- Plate with green onion, using salt and pepper to taste

- **Four-Ingredient Granola Bars**
-
- **What's in it:**
-
- 3 tbsp. water
- ¾ c. dried cranberries
- 2 c. desiccated coconut
- 2 c. walnuts
- 1 c. pitted dates
-
- **How it's made:**
-
- Preheat over to 170 degrees then proceed to toast walnuts. Let cool before putting in a food processor. Add in cranberries, coconut, and dates
- Mix until well combined and crumbly
- Add water one tablespoon at a time, creating a mixture sticky in texture that is able to hold together
- Line cling wrap in a baking dish, preferably square and then press the mixture inside it
- Place inside fridge for a couple to few hours
- Sprinkle with coconut and cut into bars
-

Whole Lunch Recipes

Sausage and Kale Sauté

What's in it:

- ½ of a chopped red bell pepper
- 1 diced onion
- 1 bunch kale
- 1 pound sausage

How it's made:

- In a large pan, brown sausage
- Add onion in pan and cook until they are soft and translucent in color
- Remove kale spine and chop into bite sized pieces
- Add kale to pan. Cook and stir until kale leaves are bright green in color and is a texture you prefer
- Remove kale and sausage mixture from the pan and stir in red pepper. Serve while warm

Turkey Plantain Nachos

What's in it:

- 2 c. lettuce, shredded
- 1 6 oz. bag plantain chips
- 2 tbsp. taco seasoning
- 1 pound of lean ground turkey
- Other toppings: guacamole, salsa, tomatoes, peppers, onions, etc.

- **How it's made:**
-
- Brown turkey in a skillet
- While turkey is cooking, prepare toppings
- Once turkey is cooked, add taco seasoning and stir until combined.
- Place plantain chips on bottom, then lettuce, turkey, and other toppings in an order that your taste buds prefer. Enjoy!
-
-
-
-
-
-
-
-
-
-
-
-

Whole Dinner Recipes

Roasted Lemon Chicken with Potatoes

What's in it:

- ½ tsp. salt and pepper
- ½ tsp. red pepper flakes
- 1 tbsp. rosemary
- 2 cloves garlic
- 1/3 c. olive oil
- 2 lemons, sliced and juiced
- ½ onion
- 1 pound baby red potatoes
- 8-10 pieces of chicken with skin on and bone in

How it's made:

- Ensure oven is preheated to 400 degrees
- Prime 1 13x9 glass baking dish with cooking spray. Place pieces of chicken with skin side up with potatoes, cut up onion and lemon slices, ensuring that all ingredients are even in pan
- Mix together lemon juice, red pepper flakes, salt, pepper, rosemary and garlic in a small bowl
- Pour this mixture over the chicken, tossing to ensure even coating
- Sprinkle with pepper and salt
- Bake chicken, uncover, for an hour or until cooked

- **Tomato Basil Beef Goulash with Eggplant**
-
- **What's in it:**
-
- ¾ c. coconut cream
- 2 tbsp. tomato paste
- 2 tsp. salt
- 1/3 c. basil
- 1 14 oz. can diced tomatoes
- 1 eggplant
- 1 pound ground beef
- 4 garlic gloves
- 2 shallots
- 2 tbsp. olive oil
-
- **How it's made:**
-
- In a large saucepan, heat olive oil, then add garlic and shallots. Sauté until fragrant
- Add in beef and cook until browned
- In another pan, heat more olive oil and pour in eggplant, cooking until soft
- Once beef is cooked, drain grease and add tomatoes, salt, and basil. Stir until well-combined, then add in coconut cream, eggplant and tomato paste
- Serve with garnish and more basil
-
-
-
-

Whole Dessert Recipes

Banana, Cinnamon, and Nutmeg Ice Cream

What's in it:

- Cinnamon and nutmeg
- ½ c. coconut milk
- 1 c. frozen bananas

How it's made:

Place all ingredients into a blender until combined. If too thick, add more coconut milk.
Enjoy!

Coconut Almond Butter Truffles

What's in it:

- ¼ tsp. almond extract
- Pinch of salt
- 2 tbsp. almond butter
- ¼ c. coconut butter

Optional:

- ½ tbsp. coconut oil
- 1 tsp. unsweetened cocoa powder

How it's made:

- In a small bowl, mix together almond butter and coconut and warm in microwave until melted, stirring until smooth in texture
- Add almond extract and salt and stir
- Freeze for around 10 minutes until hardened
- After freezing, roll into balls and then return back to freezing
- In a small bowl, melt coconut oil and stir in cocoa powder until combined. Dip balls into mixture of chocolate and let chocolate set. Re-dip for thicker coating and let sit until set.
- Keep in fridge if all of them aren't eaten at once!
-
- **Raw Brownie Bites**
-
- **What's in it:**
-
- 1/3 c. unsweetened cocoa powder
- 1 tsp. vanilla
- 1 c. pitted dates
- Pinch of salt
- 1 ½ c. walnuts
-
- **How it's made:**
-
- In a food processor, finely grind walnuts and salt
- Add cocoa powder, vanilla and dates into food processor. Mix until everything is combined. Add water a little at a time until you have a mixture that sticks together
- Put mixture into a bowl. Use hands and form small balls. Store in container within the fridge for up to one week.
-

-
-
-
-
-
-
-
-
-
-
-
-
-
-

-
- Conclusion
-
- Thank for making it through to the end of *30 Day Whole Foods Cookbook: The Only 30 Days You Ever Need to Great Health.* I hope that you found the contents of this book is everything you needed to get started on incorporating the Whole Diet directly into your lifestyle as soon as possible!

- The contents of this cookbook should have provided you with all the necessary tools to achieve your goals to a better diet plan. You have within your hands the perfect vessel to lead you to a path of healthier eating, with the perfect amount of meals and other recipes to get you started on the right foot!

- Isn't it about time that you took the initiative to feel better about yourself inside AND out? Wouldn't it be an amazing feeling to have the energy to do all the things you love every day?

Isn't it about time that you took the initiative to healthier living today rather than waiting until tomorrow?

- The next step is to put the rules of the Whole Diet to work for you, starting with making the delicious recipes that are included in the contents of this book! All these recipes go great with your other favorite eats, as well as paired with other recipes that are within the chapters of this cookbook!

- I hope that the contents of this cookbook will help you gain the confidence to start incorporating healthier lifestyle habits within your everyday life today!

-
-
-
-
-
-
-
-
-

BOOK TWO

THE 10 DAY KETOGENIC CLEANSE

INCREASE YOUR METABOLISM AND DETOX WITH THESE DELICIOUS AND FUN IN A FAST 10 DAY MEAL PLAN

DIANA WATSON

- DEDICATION
  -
  -
  -
  -
  -
  -
  -
  -
  -
  -
  -
  -
  -
  -
  -
  -
  -
  -
  -
  -
  -
  -

-

CONTENTS

ACKNOWLEDGMENTS

INTRODUCTION

Hello, dear reader! We are immensely thankful you are interested in improving your health and fitness by utilizing the methods involved in a ketogenic diet. It is our hope that your determination combined with our thorough meal plan and wonderful recipes will give you a jump start toward your fitness goals. You may have opened this book with a question in mind, "What in the world is a ketogenic cleanse, anyway?" Well, we are glad you asked! A ketogenic cleanse is inspired by the methods of a ketogenic diet. A ketogenic diet aims to change your body's metabolic focus from carbohydrate- based to fat-based fuels in order to produce cellular energy. Its aim is to develop healthy eating habits by replacing useless foods with the nutrients and fuel your body actually needs. This book contains further information about ketogenic dieting and a ten day meal plan accompanied by easy recipes. Having access to a meal plan is one of the most effective ways you can stay motivated along your ketogenic diet journey. So put on your apron, grab your greens, and head to the kitchen for some fat burning, healthy living!

CHAPTER 1: KETO BASICS

In the introduction we briefly discussed the meaning and theory behind ketogenic dieting. Here we will delve further into the science behind the method and how it can boost your metabolism and detox your body in 10 days.

BENEFITS OF INCREASED METABOLISM

One of the best ways to learn the meaning of a scientific term is to break it down to its roots. When we break down ketogenic we see it is comprised of two words: keto and genic. Ketones are fat-based molecules that the body breaks down when it is using fat as its energy source. When used as a suffix, "genic" means "causing, forming, or producing". So, we put these terms together and we have "ketogenic", or simply put, "causing fat burn". Ergo, the theory behind ketogenic dieting is: when a person reduces the amount of sugar and carbohydrates they consume, the body will begin to breakdown fat it already has in stores all over the body. When your body is cashing in on these stores, it is in a ketogenic state, or "ketosis". When your body consumes food, it naturally seeks carbohydrates for the purpose of breaking them down and using them as fuel. Adversely, a ketogenic cleanse trains your body to use fats for energy instead. This is achieved by lowering the amount of ingested carbohydrates and increasing the amount of ingested fats, which in turn boosts your metabolism.

Only recently has a low carb- high fat diet plan
emerged into the public eye. It is a sharp contrast to
the traditional dieting style that emphasizes calorie
counting. For many years it was over looked that
crash diets neglect the most important aspect of
dieting: food is fuel. A diet is not meant be treated
as a once a year go to method in order to shed
holiday weight in January. Rather, a diet is a
lifestyle; it is a consistent pattern of how an
individual fuels their body. A ten day ketogenic
cleanse is the perfect way to begin forming healthy
eating habits that overtime become second nature.
If you are tired of losing weight just to gain it all
back, never fear. We firmly believe that you can
accomplish anything you put your mind to, including
living a healthy life! You, like hundreds of others,
can successfully accomplish a ketogenic cleanse and

change the way you see health, fitness, and life along the way. So let's hit the books and get that metabolism working!

BENEFITS OF CLEANSING

In addition to increased metabolism and fat loss, ketogenic cleansing allows your body naturally rid itself of harmful toxins and wasteful substances. In today's modern world, food is overrun and polluted by genetically modified hormones, artificial flavors and coloring, and copious amounts of unnecessary sugars. Ketogenic cleansing eliminates breads, grains, and many other foods that are most affected by today's modern industrialization. Due to the high amount of naturally occurring foods used in a ketogenic cleanse, the body is able to obtain many vitamins and minerals that are not prevalent in a high carb diet. When the body is consuming sufficient amounts of necessary vitamins and minerals, it is able to heal itself and maintain a healthy immune system. Cleansing your body is one of the best ways to achieve, and maintain, pristine health.

CHAPTER 2: MEAL PLAN MADNESS

One of the best ways to stay motivated, when dieting, is to find a meal plan that is easy to follow and easy on the budget. Ketogenic meals are designed to be filling while keeping within the perimeters of low-carb, high-fat guidelines. Ideally you want to aim for 70% fats, 25% protein, and 5% carbohydrates in your diet. As long as the materials you use to build your meals are low in carbs and high in fats, feel free to experiment and find what is right for you. Each and every one of us is different and that's okay. After all, this meal plan is for YOU!

Below is a ten day meal plan, designed with a busy schedule in mind, which will not break the bank! All of these meals can be prepared in 30 minutes or less, and many of them are much quicker than that! There is also a list of ingredients for each meal located in the recipe chapter so you can go to the grocery store knowing exactly what you need!

	Breakfast	Lunch	Dinner
Day 1	**California Chicken Omelet** • Fat: 32 grams • 10 minutes to prepare • Protein: 25 grams • 10 minutes of cooking • Net carbs: 4 grams •	**Cobb Salad** • Fat: 48 grams • 10 minutes to prepare • Protein: 43 grams • 0 minutes of cooking • Net carbs: 3 grams •	**Chicken Peanut Pad Thai** • Fat: 12 grams • 15 minutes to prepare • Protein: 30 grams • 15 minutes of cooking • Net carbs: 2 grams
Day 2	**Easy Blender Pancakes** • Fat: 29	**Sardine Stuffed Avocados** • Fat: 29 grams	**Chipotle Fish Tacos** • Fat: 20 grams • 5

	grams • 5 minutes to prepare • Protein: 41 grams • 10 minutes of cooking • Net carbs: 4 grams	• 10 minutes to prepare • Protein: 27 grams • 0 minutes of cooking • Net Carbs: 5 grams	minutes to prepare • Protein: 24 grams • 15 minutes of cooking • Net carbs: 5 grams
Day 3	**Steak and Eggs** • Fat: 36 grams • 10 minutes to prepare • Protein:	**Low-Carb Smoothie Bowl** • Fat 35 grams • 5 minutes to prepare • Protein: 20 grams • 0 minutes	**Avocado Lime Salmon** • Fat: 27 grams • 20 minutes to prepare • Protein: 37 grams • 10 minutes of

	• 47 grams • 5 minutes of cooking • Net carbs: 3 grams	of cooking • Net carbs: 5 grams	cooking • Net carbs: 5 grams •
KEEP IT UP!!!	During the course of your plan, especially around days 3 and 4, you may begin to feel like you don't have it in you. You may have thoughts telling you that you cannot last for ten days on this type pf cleanse. Do not allow feelings of discouragement bother you because, guess what? We all feel that way sometimes! A ketogenic diet causes your body to process energy like it never has before. Keep pressing on! Your body will thank you and so will you!		
Day 4	**Low-Carb Smoothie Bowl** • Fat: 35 grams • 5 minutes to prepare • Protein: 35 grams • 0 minutes of cooking • Net carbs: 4 grams	**Pesto Chicken Salad** • Fat: 27 grams • 5 minutes to prepare • Prote	**Siracha Lime Flank Steak** • Fat: 32 grams • 5 minutes to prepare • are

		in: 27 grams	• Prote in: 48 gram s
		• 10 minu tes of cooki ng • Net carbs : 3 gram s	• 10 minu tes of cooki ng • Net Carb s: 5 gram s
Day 5	**Feta and Pesto Omelet** • Fat: 46 grams • 5 minutes of preparation • Protein: 30 grams • 5 minutes of cooking • Net carbs: 2.5 grams	**Roasted Brussel Sprouts** • Fat: 21 gram s • 5 minu tes to prep are • Prote in: 21 gram s • 30 minu tes of cooki ng	**Low carb Sesame Chicken** • Fat: 36 gram s • 15 minu tes to prep are • Prote in: 41 gram s • 15 minu tes of cooki ng • Net carbs

		• Net carbs : 4 grams	: 4 grams
Day 6	**Raspberry Cream Crepes** • Fat: 40 grams • 5 minutes of preparation • Net carbs: 8 grams • 15 minutes of cooking • Protein 15 grams	**Shakshuka** • Fat: 34 grams • Protein 35 grams • Net carbs : 4 grams • 10 minutes of preparation • 10 minutes of cooking	**Sausage in a Pan** • Fat: 38 grams • 10 minutes of preparation • Protein: 30 grams • 25 minutes of cooking • Net Carbs : 4 grams
Day 7	**Green Monster Smoothie** • Fat: 25 grams • 5 minutes of preparation	**Tuna Tartare** • Fat: 24 grams • 15	**Pesto Chicken Salad** • Fat: 27 grams

35

	• Protein: 30 grams • 0 minutes of cooking • Net Carbs: 3 grams	minu tes of prep arati on • Prote in: 56 gram s • 0 minu tes of cooki ng • Net Carb s: 4 gram s •	• 5 minu tes of prep arati on • Prote in: 27 gram s • 10 minu tes of cooki ng • Net carbs : 3 gram s
ALM OST THER E!!	By now, you can be certain you are seeing physical results such as reduced body fat and more energy! You are doing a fantastic job and you only have three days left! Keep up the good work, you owe it to yourself.		
Day 8	**Shakshuk a** • Fat: 34 gram s • 10 minu tes of prep arati	**Grilled Halloumi Salad** • Fat: 47 grams • 15 minutes of preparation • Protein: 21 grams • 0 minutes of cooking • Net carbs: 2	**Keto Quarter Pounder** • Fat: 34 gram s • 10 minu tes of prep arati

		grams	
	• Prote in 35 gram s • 10 minu tes of cooki ng • Net carbs : 4 gram s	•	• on Prote in: 25 gram s • 8 minu tes of cooki ng • Net carbs : 4 •
Day 9	**Easy Blender Pancakes** • Fat: 29 gram s • 5 minu tes of prep arati on • Prote in: 41 gram s • 10 minu tes	**Broccoli Bacon Salad** • Fat: 31 grams • 15 minutes of preparation • Protein: 10 grams • 6 minutes of cooking • Net carbs: 5 grams	**Sardine Stuffed Avocados** • Fat: 29 gram s • 10 minu tes to prep are • Prote in: 27 gram s • 0 minu tes to cook • Net

	of cooking • Net carbs : 4 grams		Carbs: 5 grams
Day 10	**California Chicken Omelet** • Fat 32 grams • 10 minutes to prepare • Protein 25 grams • 10 minutes of cooking • Net carb: 3 grams •	**Shrimp Scampi** • Fat: 21 grams • 5 minutes to prepare • Protein: 21 grams • 30 minutes of cooking • Net carbs: 4 grams	**Tuna Tartare** • Fat: 36 grams • 15 minutes to prepare • Protein: 41 grams • 15 minutes of cooking • Net carbs : 4 grams
YOU	Congratulations! You have successfully		

DID **IT!!**	completed a 10 day ketogenic cleanse. By now your body has adjusted to its new source of energy, expelled dozens of harmful toxins, and replenished itself with many vitamins and minerals it may have been lacking. Way to go on a job well done!

CHAPTER 3: BREAKFAST IS FOR CHAMPIONS

Breakfast is by far the most important meal of the day for one reason: it set the tone for the rest of your day. In order to hit the ground running, it is vital that one starts each day with foods that fuel an energetic and productive day. This chapter contains ten ketogenic breakfast ides that will have you burning fat and conquering your day like you never imagined.

1. CALIFORNIA CHICKEN OMELET
- This recipe requires 10 minutes of preparation, 10 minutes of

cooking time and serves 1

- Net carbs: 4 grams

- Protein: 25 grams

- Fat : 32 grams

• What you will need:

- Mayo (1 tablespoon)

- Mustard (1 teaspoon)

- Campari tomato

- Eggs (2 large beaten)

- Avocado (one fourth, sliced)

- Bacon (2 slices cooked and chopped)

- Deli chicken (1 ounce)

- What to do:

1. Place a skillet on the stove over a burner set to a medium heat and let it warm before adding in the eggs and seasoning as needed.

2. Once eggs are cooked about halfway through, add bacon, chicken, avocado, tomato, mayo, and mustard on one side of the eggs.

3. Fold the omelet onto its self, cover and cook for 5 additional minutes.

4. Once eggs are fully cooked and all ingredients are warm, through the center, your omelet is ready.

5. Bon apatite!

6.

7. 2. STEAK AND EGGS WITH AVOCADO

- This recipe requires 10 minutes of preparation, 5 minutes of cooking time and serves 1

- Net Carbs: 3 grams

- Protein: 44 grams

- Fat: 36 grams

- ## What you will need:

- Salt and pepper

- Avocado (one fourth, sliced)

- Sirloin steak (4 ounce)

- Eggs (3 large)

- Butter (1 tablespoon)

- ## What to do:

1. Melt the tablespoon of butter in a pan and fry all 3 eggs to desired doneness. Season the eggs with salt and pepper.

2. In a different pan, cook the sirloin steak to your preferred taste and slice it into thin strips. Season the steak with salt and pepper.

3. Sever your prepared steak and eggs with slices of avocado.

4. Enjoy!

5.

6. 3. PANCAKES IN A BLENDER

- This recipe requires 5 minutes of preparation, 10 minutes of cooking time and serves 1

- Net Carbs: 4 grams

- Protein: 41 grams

- Fat: 29 grams

• What you will need:

- Whey protein powder (1 scoop)

- Eggs (2 large)

- Cream cheese (2 ounces)

- Just a pinch of cinnamon and a pinch of salt

- What to do:

1. Combine cream cheese, eggs, protein powder, cinnamon, and salt into a blender. Blend for 10 seconds and let stand.

2. While letting batter stand, warm a skillet over medium heat.

3. Pour about ¼ of the batter onto warmed skillet and let cook.

When bubbles begin to emerge on the surface, flip the pancake.

4. Once flipped, cook for 15 seconds. Repeat until remainder of the batter is used up.

5. Top with butter and/ or sugar- free maple syrup and you are all set!

6. Chow time!

7.

8. ## 4. LOW CARB SMOOTHE BOWL

- Net Carbs: 4 grams

- Protein: 35 grams

- Fat: 35 grams

- Takes 5 minutes to prepare and serves 1.

- ## What you will need:

- Spinach (1 cup)

- Almond milk (half a cup)

- Coconut oil (1 tablespoon)

- Low carb protein powder (1 scoop)

- Ice cubes (2 cubes)

- Whipping cream (2 T)

- Optional toppings can include: raspberries, walnuts, shredded coconut, or chia seeds

- What to do:

1. Place spinach in blender. Add almond milk, cream, coconut oil, and ice. Blend until thoroughly and evenly combined.

2. Pour into bowl.

3. Top with toppings or stir lightly into smoothie.

4. Treat yourself!

5.

6. **5. FETA AND PESTO OMELET**

- This recipe requires 5 minutes of preparation, 5 minutes of cooking time and serves 1

- Net Carbs: 2.5 grams

- Protein: 30 grams

- Fat: 46 grams

• What you will need:

- Butter (1 tablespoon)

- Eggs (3 large)

- Heavy cream (1 tablespoon)

- Feta cheese (1 ounce)

- Basil pesto (1 teaspoon)

- Tomatoes (optional)

- What to do:

1. Heat pan and melt butter.

2. Beat eggs together with heavy whipping cream (will give eggs a fluffy consistency once cooked).

3. Pour eggs in pan and cook until almost done, add feta and pesto to on half of eggs.

4. Fold omelet and cook for an additional 4-5 minutes.

5. Top with feta and tomatoes, and eat up!

6. ## 6. CREPES WITH CREAM AND RASPBERRIES
- This recipe requires 5 minutes of preparation, 15 minutes of cooking time and serves 2

- Net Carbs: 8 grams

- Protein: 15 grams

- Fat: 40 grams

• What you will need:

- Raspberries (3 ounces, fresh or frozen)

- Whole Milk Ricotta (half a cup and 2 tablespoons)

- Erythritol (2 tablespoons)

- Eggs (2 large)

- Cream Cheese (2 ounces)

- Pinch of salt

- Dash of Cinnamon

- Whipped cream and sugar- free maple syrup to go on top

- What to do:

1. In a blender, blend cream cheese, eggs, erythritol, salt, and cinnamon for about 20 seconds, or until there are no lumps of cream cheese.

2. Place a pan on a burner turned to a medium heat before coating in cooking spray. Add 20 percent of your batter to the pan in a thin layer. Cook crepe until the underside becomes slightly darkened. Carefully flip the crepe and let the reverse side cook for about 15 seconds.

3. Repeat step 3 until all batter is used.

4. Without stacking the crepes, allow them to cool for a few minutes.

5. After the crepes have cool, place about 2 tablespoons of ricotta cheese in the center of each crepe.

6. Throw in a couple of raspberries and fold the side to the middle.

7. Top those off with some whipped cream and sugar- free maple syrup and...

8. Viola! You're a true chef! Indulge in your creation!

9.

- This recipe requires 10 minutes of preparation, 0 minutes of cooking time and serves 1

- Net Carbs: 4 grams

- Protein: 30 grams

- Fat: 25 grams

- ## What you will need:

- Almond milk (one and a half cups)

- Spinach (one eighth of a cup)

- Cucumber (fourth of a cup)

- Celery (fourth of a cup)

- Avocado (fourth of a cup)

- Coconut oil (1 tablespoon)

- Stevia (liquid, 10 drops)

- Whey Protein Powder (1 scoop)

- ## What to do:

1. In a blender, blend almond milk and spinach for a few pulses.

2. Add remaining ingredients and blend until thoroughly

combined.

3. Add optional matcha powder, if desired, and enjoy!

4.

5.

6.

7.

8.

9.

10.

11.

12.

13.

14.

15.

16.

17.

18.

19.

20. CHAPTER 4: LUNCH CRUNCH

21. Eating a healthy lunch when you are limited
on time due to, work, school, or taking care of
your kids can be a tumultuous task.
Thankfully, we have compiled a list of eight

quick and easy recipes to accompany the ten day meal plan laid out in chapter 2! Many find it advantageous, especially if you work throughout the week, to prepare you meals ahead of time. Thankfully, these lunch recipes are also easy to pack and take on the go!

22.

23. 1. OFF THE COBB SALAD

- Net carbs: 3 grams

- Protein: 43 grams

- Fat: 48 grams

- Takes 10 minutes to prepare and serves 1.

- What you will need:

- Spinach (1 cup)

- Egg (1, hard-boiled)

- Bacon (2 strips)

- Chicken breast (2 ounces)

- Campari tomato (one half of tomato)

- Avocado (one fourth, sliced)

- White vinegar (half of a teaspoon)

- Olive oil (1 tablespoon)

- What to do:

1. Cook chicken and bacon completely and cut or slice into small pieces.

2. Chop remaining ingredients into bite size pieces.

3. Place all ingredients, including chicken and bacon, in a bowl, toss ingredients in oil and vinegar.

4. Enjoy!

5.

6. 2. AVOCADO AND SARDINES

- Net Carbs: 5 grams

- Protein: 27 grams

- Fat: 52 grams

- Takes 10 minutes to prepare and serves 1.

- ## What you will need:

- Fresh lemon juice (1 tablespoon)

- Spring onion or chives (1 or small bunch)

- Mayonnaise (1 tablespoon)

- Sardines (1 tin, drained)

- Avocado (1 whole, seed removed)

- Turmeric powder (fourth of a teaspoon) or freshly ground turmeric root (1 teaspoon)

- Salt (fourth of a teaspoon)

- ## What to do:

1. Begin by cutting the avocado in half and removing its seed.

2. Scoop out about half the avocado and set aside (shown below).

3.
4.

5. In small bowl, mash drained sardines with fork.

6. Add onion (or chives), turmeric powder, and mayonnaise. Mix well.

7. Add removed avocado to sardine mixture.

8. Add lemon juice and salt.

9. Scoop the mixture into avocado halves.

10. Dig in!

11.

12.
13. 3. CHICKEN SALAD A LA PESTO

- This recipe requires 5minutes of preparation, 10 minutes of cooking time and serves 4

- Net Carbs: 3 grams

- Protein: 27 grams

- Fat: 27 grams

- ## What you will need:

- Garlic pesto (2 tablespoons)

- Mayonnaise (fourth of a cup)

- Grape tomatoes (10, halved)

- Avocado (1, cubed)

- Bacon (6 slices, cooked crisp and crumbled)

- Chicken (1 pound, cooked and cubed)

- Romaine lettuce (optional)

- ## What to do:

1. Combine all ingredients in a large mixing bowl.

2. Toss gently to spread mayonnaise and pesto evenly throughout.

3. If desired, wrap in romaine lettuce for a low-carb BLT chicken wrap.

4. Bon apatite!

5.

6. 4. BACON AND ROASTED BRUSSEL

SPROUTS

- This recipe requires 5 minutes of preparation, 30 minutes of cooking time and serves 4

- Net Carbs: 4 grams

- Protein: 15 grams

- Fat: 21 grams

- What you will need:

- Bacon (8 strips)

- Olive oil (2 tablespoons)

- Brussel sprouts (1 pound, halved)

- Salt and pepper

- What to do:

1. Preheat oven to 375 degrees Fahrenheit.

2. Gently mix Brussel sprouts with olive oil, salt, and pepper.

3. Spread Brussel sprouts evenly onto a greased baking sheet.

4. Bake in oven for 30 minutes. Shake the pan about halfway through to mix the Brussel sprout halves up a bit.

5. While Brussel sprouts are in the oven, fry bacon slices on stovetop.

6. When bacon is fully cooked, let cool and chop it into bite size pieces.

7. Combine bacon and Brussel sprouts in a bowl and you're finished!

8. Feast!!

9.

10. 5. GRILLED HALLOUMI SALAD

- Net Carbs: 7 grams

- Protein: 21 grams

- Fat: 47 grams

- Takes 15 minutes to prepare and serves 1.

- ## What you will need:

- Chopped walnuts (half of an ounce)

- Baby arugula (1 handful)

- Grape tomatoes (5)

- Cucumber (1)

- Halloumi cheese (3 ounces)

- Olive oil (1 teaspoon)

- Balsamic vinegar (half of a teaspoon)

- A pinch of salt

- ## What to do:

1. Slice halloumi cheese into slices 1/3 of an in thick.

2. Grill cheese for 3 to 5 minutes, until you see grill lines, on

each side.

3. Wash and cut veggies into bite size pieces, place in salad bowl.

4. Add rinsed baby arugula and walnuts to veggies.

5. Toss in olive oil, balsamic vinegar, and salt.

6. Place grilled halloumi on top of veggies and your lunch is ready!

7. Eat those greens and get back to work!

8.

9.
10. **6. BACON BROCCOLI SALAD**

- This recipe requires 15 minutes of preparation, 6 minutes of cooking time and serves 5.

- Net Carbs: 5 grams

- Protein: 10 grams

- Fat: 31 grams

- ## What you will need:

- Sesame oil (half of a teaspoon)

- Erythritol (1 and a half tablespoons) or stevia to taste

- White vinegar (1 tablespoon)

- Mayonnaise (half of a cup)

- Green onion (three fourths of an ounce)

- Bacon (fourth of a pound)

- Broccoli (1 pound, heads and stalks cut and trimmed)

- ## What to do:

1. Cook bacon and crumble into bits.

2. Cut broccoli into bite sized pieces.

3. Slice scallions.

4. Mix mayonnaise, vinegar, erythritol (or stevia), and sesame oil, to make the dressing.

5. Place broccoli and bacon bits in a bowl and toss with dressing.

6. Viola!

7.

8. **7. TUNA AVOCADO TARTARE**

- Net Carbs: 4 grams

- Protein: 56 grams

- Fat: 24 grams

- Takes 15 minutes to prepare and serves 2.

- ## What you will need:

- Sesame seed oil (2 tablespoons)

- Sesame seeds (1 teaspoon)

- Cucumbers (2)

- Lime (half of a whole lime)

- Mayonnaise (1 tablespoon)

- Sriracha (1 tablespoon)

- Olive oil (2 tablespoons)

- Jalapeno (one half of whole jalapeno)

- Scallion (3 stalks)

- Avocado (1)

- Tuna steak (1 pound)

- Soy sauce (1 tablespoon)

- What to do:

1. Dice tuna and avocado into ¼ inch cubes, place in bowl.

2. Finely chop scallion and jalapeno, add to bowl.

3. Pour olive oil, sesame oil, siracha, soy sauce, mayonnaise, and lime into bowl.

4. Using hands, toss all ingredients to combine evenly. Using a utensil may breakdown avocado, which you want to remain chunky, so it is best to use your hands.

5. Top with sesame seeds and serve with a side of sliced cucumber.

6. There's certainly something fishy about this recipe, but it tastes great! Enjoy!

7.

8. **8. WARM SPINACH AND SHRIMP**

- This recipe requires 15 minutes of preparation, 6 minutes of cooking time and serves 5.

- Fat: 24 grams

- Protein: 36 grams

- Net Carbs: 3 grams

- Takes10 minutes to prepare, 5 minutes to cook, and serves 2.

- ## What you will need:

- Spinach (2 handfuls)

- Parmesan (half a tablespoon)

- Heavy cream (1 tablespoon)

- Olive oil (1 tablespoon)

- Butter (2 tablespoons)

- Garlic (3 cloves)

- Onion (one fourth of whole onion)

- Large raw shrimp (about 20)

- Lemon (optional)

What to do:

1. Place peeled shrimp in cold water.

2. Chop onions and garlic into fine pieces.

3. Heat oil, in pan, over medium heat. Cook shrimp in oil until lightly pink (we do not want them fully cooked here). Remove shrimp from oil and set aside.

4. Place chopped onions and garlic into pan, cook until onions are translucent. Add a dash of salt.

5. Add butter, cream, and parmesan cheese. Stir until you have a smooth sauce.

6. Let sauce cook for about 2 minutes so it will thicken slightly.

7. Place shrimp back into pan and cook until done. This should take no longer than 2 or 3 minutes. Be careful not to overcook the shrimp, it will become dry and tough!

8. Remove shrimp and sauce from pan and replace with spinach. Cook spinach VERY briefly

9. Place warmed spinach onto a plate.

10. Pour shrimp and sauce over bed of spinach, squeeze some lemon on top, if you like, and you're ready to chow down!

11.

12.

13. CHAPTER 5: THINNER BY DINNER

14. It's the end of the day and you are winding down from a hard day's work. Your body does not require a lot of energy while you sleep; therefore, dinner will typically consist of less fat and more protein.

15.

16. 1. CHICKEN PAD THAI

- Net Carbs: 7 grams

- Protein: 30 grams

- Fat: 12 grams

- Takes 15 minutes to prepare, 15 minutes to cook, and serves 4.

- What you will need:

- Peanuts (1 ounce)

- Lime (1 whole)

- Soy sauce (2 tablespoons)

- Egg (1 large)

- Zucchini (2 large)

- Chicken thighs (16 ounces, boneless and skinless)

- Garlic (2 cloves, minced)
- White onion (1,chopped)
- Olive oil (1 tablespoon)
- Chili flakes (optional)

- What to do:

1. Over medium heat, cook olive oil and onion until translucent. Add the garlic and cook about three minutes (until fragrant).

2. Cook chicken in pan for 5 to 7 minutes on each side (until fully cooked). Remove chicken from heat and shred it using a couple of forks.

3. Cut ends off zucchini and cut into thin noodles. Set zucchini noodles aside.

4. Next, scramble the egg in the pan.

5. Once the egg is fully cooked, and the zucchini noodles and cook for about 2 minutes.

6. Add the previously shredded chicken to the pan.

7. Give it some zing with soy sauce, lime juice, peanuts, and chili flakes.

8. Time to eat!

9.
10. 2. CHIPOTLE STYLE FISH TACOS

- Fat: 20 grams

- Protein: 24 grams

- Net Carbs: 7 grams

- Takes 5 minutes to prepare, 15 minutes to cook, and serves 4.

- ## What you will need:

- Low carb tortillas (4)

- Haddock fillets (1 pound)

- Mayonnaise (2 tablespoons)

- Butter (2 tablespoons)

- Chipotle peppers in adobo sauce (4 ounces)

- Garlic (2 cloves, pressed)

- Jalapeño (1 fresh, chopped)

- Olive oil (2 tablespoons)

- Yellow onion (half of an onion, diced)

- ## What to do:

1. Fry diced onion (until translucent) in olive oil in a high sided pan, over medium- high heat.

2. Reduce heat to medium, add jalapeno and garlic. Cook while stir for another two minutes.

3. Chop the chipotle peppers and add them, along with the adobo sauce, to the pan.

4. Add the butter, mayo, and fish fillets to the pan.

5. Cook the fish fully while breaking up the fillets and stirring the fish into other ingredients.

6. Warm tortillas for 2 minutes on each side.

7. Fill tortillas with fishy goodness and eat up!

8.

9. **3. SALMON WITH AVOCADO LIME SAUCE**

- Net Carbs: 5 grams

- Protein: 37 grams

- Fat: 27 grams

- Takes 20 minutes to prepare, 10 minutes to cook, and serves 2.

- What you will need:

- Salmon (two 6 ounce fillets)

- Avocado (1 large)

- Lime (one half of a whole lime)

- Red onion (2 tablespoons, diced)

- Cauliflower (100 grams)

- What to do:

1. Chop cauliflower in a blender or food processor then cook it in a lightly oiled pan, while covered, for 8 minutes. This will make the cauliflower rice-like.

2. Next, blend the avocado with squeezed lime juice in the blender or processor until smooth and creamy.

3. Heat some oil in a skillet and cook salmon (skin side down

first) for 4 to 5 minute. Flip the fillets and cook for an additional 4 to 5 minutes.

4. Place salmon fillet on a bed of your cauliflower rice and top with some diced red onion.

5. **4. SIRACHA LIME STEAK**
- Net Carbs: 5 grams

- Protein: 48 grams

- Fat: 32 grams

- Takes 5 minutes to prepare, 10 minutes to cook, and serves 2.

- What you will need:

- Vinegar (1 teaspoon)

- Olive oil (2 tablespoons)

- Lime (1 whole)

- Sriracha (2 tablespoons)

- Flank steak (16 ounce)

- Salt and pepper

- What to do:

1. Season steak, liberally, with salt and pepper. Place on baking sheet, lined with foil, and broil in oven for 5 minutes on each side (add another minute or two for a well done steak). Remove from oven, cover, and set aside.

2. Place sriracha in small bowl and squeeze lime into it. Whisk in salt, pepper, and vinegar.

3. Slowly pour in olive oil.

4. Slice steak into thin slices, lather on your sauce, and enjoy!

5. Feel free to pair this recipe with a side of greens such as asparagus or broccoli.

6. ## 5. LOW CARB SESAME CHICKEN

- Net Carbs: 4 grams

- Protein: 45 grams

- Fat: 36 grams

- Takes 15minutes to prepare, 15 minutes to cook, and serves 2.

- ## What you will need:

- Broccoli (three fourths of a cup, cut bite size)

- Xanthan gum (fourth of a teaspoon)

- Sesame seeds (2 tablespoons)

- Garlic (1 clove)

- Ginger (1 cm cube)

- Vinegar (1 tablespoon)

- Brown sugar alternative (Sukrin Gold is a good one) (2 tablespoons)

- Soy sauce (2 tablespoons)

- Toasted sesame seed oil (2 tablespoons)

- Arrowroot powder or corn starch (1 tablespoon)

- Chicken thighs (1poundcut into bite sized pieces)

- Egg (1 large)

- Salt and pepper

- Chives (optional)

- ## What to do:

1. First we will make the batter by combining the egg with a tablespoon of arrowroot powder (or cornstarch). Whisk well.

2. Place chicken pieces in batter. Be sure to coat all sides of chicken pieces with the batter.

3. Heat one tablespoon of sesame oil, in a large pan. Add chicken pieces to hot oil and fry. Be gentle when flipping the chicken, you want to keep the batter from falling off. It should take about 10 minutes for them to cook fully.

4. Next, make the sesame sauce. In a small bowl, combine soy sauce, brown sugar alternative, vinegar, ginger, garlic, sesame seeds, and the remaining tablespoon of toasted sesame seed oil. Whisk very well.

5. Once the chicken is fully cooked, add broccoli and the sesame sauce to pan and cook for an additional 5 minutes.

6. Spoon desired amount into a bowl, top it off with some chopped chives, and relish in some fine dining at home!

7. 6. PAN 'O SAUSAGE

- Net Carbs: 4 grams

- Protein: 30 grams

- Fat: 38 grams

- Takes 10 minutes to prepare, 25 minutes to cook, and serves 2.

- What you will need:

- Basil (half a teaspoon)

- Oregano (half a teaspoon)

- White onion (1 tablespoon)

- Shredded mozzarella (fourth of a cup)

- Parmesan cheese (fourth of a cup)

- Vodka sauce (half a cup)

- Mushrooms (4 ounces)

- Sausage (3 links)

- Salt (fourth of a teaspoon)

- Red pepper (fourth of a teaspoon, ground)

- What to do:

1. Preheat oven to 350 degrees Fahrenheit.

2. Heat an iron skillet over medium flame. When skillet is hot, cook sausage links until almost thoroughly cooked.

3. While sausage is cooking, slice mushrooms and onion.

4. When sausage is almost fully cooked, remove links from heat and place mushrooms and onions in skillet to brown.

5. Cut sausage into pieces about ½ inch thick and place pieces in pan.

6. Season skillet contents with oregano, basil, salt, and red pepper.

7. Add vodka sauce and parmesan cheese. Stir everything together.

8. Place skillet in oven for 15 minutes. Sprinkle mozzarella on top a couple minutes before removing dish from oven.

9. Once 15 minutes is up, remove skillet from the oven and let cool for a few minutes.

10. Dinner time!

11.

12. 7. QUARTER POUNDER KETO BURGER

- Net Carbs: 4 grams

- Protein: 25 grams

- Fat: 34 grams

- Takes 10 minutes to prepare, 8 minutes to cook, and serves 2.

- What you will need:

- Basil (half a teaspoon)

- Cayenne (fourth a teaspoon)

- Crushed red pepper (half a teaspoon)

- Salt (half a teaspoon)

- Lettuce (2 large leaves)

- Butter (2 tablespoons)

- Egg (1 large)

- Sriracha (1 tablespoon)

- Onion (fourth of whole onion)

- Plum tomato (half of whole tomato)

- Mayo (1 tablespoon)

- Pickled jalapenos (1 tablespoon, sliced)

- Bacon (1 strip)

- Ground beef (half a pound)

- Bacon (1 strip)

- ## What to do:

1. Knead mean for about three minute.

2. Chop bacon, jalapeno, tomato, and onion into fine pieces. (shown below)

3. Knead in mayo, sriracha, egg, and chopped ingredients, and spices into meat.

4. Separate meat into four even pieces and flatten them (not thinly, just press on the tops to create a flat surface). Place a tablespoon of butter on top of two of the meat pieces. Take the pieces that do not have butter of them and set them on top of the buttered ones (basically creating a butter and meat sandwich). Seal the sides together, concealing the butter within.

5. Throw the patties on the grill (or in a pan) for about 5 minutes on each side. Caramelize some onions if you want too!

6. Prepare large leaves of lettuce by spreading some mayo onto them. Once patties are finished, place them on one half of the

81

lettuce, add your desired burger toppings, and fold the other half over of the lettuce leaf over the patty.

7. Burger time!

8.

9. CONCLUSION

10. Thank you for purchasing this book. It is MY hope that you have had an incredible experience improving your health and learning new things while, most importantly, having fun along the way! Each and every one of us can benefit from a ketogenic cleanse and it is absolutely fantastic to witness people being conscious of their health and taking care of their bodies. Whether the 10 day ketogenic cleanse has empowered you to adopt an ongoing ketogenic diet or has shown you it is not for you, i greatly appreciate your time in reading this.

11.
12.
13. BOOK

THREE
14.
15. LOW CARB YOUR WAY TO THE PERFECT BODY
16.
17.
18. *Cut The Calories*
19. *Cut The Fat*
20.

21.

22. DIANA WATSON

25. TABLE OF CONTENTS

69.

70. INTRODUCTION

71.

72. Congratulations on purchasing your personal copy of *The Ultimate Low Carb Cookbook*. Thank you for doing so.

73. The following chapters will provide with information and recipes so that you can get started on your low carb diet journey today.

74. There are plenty of books on this subject on the market, thanks again for choosing this one! Every effort was made to ensure it is full of as much useful information as possible. Please enjoy!

75.

76.

77.

78. PERKS OF LOW CARB

79. Why in the world should you eat fewer carbs? There are many benefits for people of all ages.

80. Here are some of the main benefits of a low carb diet:

- Weight loss

- Reversing your Type 2 Diabetes

- Help Stomach Ailments

- Fewer Sugar Cravings

- Help with Blood Pressure

- Less Acne

- More Energy

- Help with Epilepsy

- Help with Heartburn

- Reverse PCOS

- Reduce ADHD Symptoms

- Staying away from carbs can result in weight loss without feeling hungry.

- Low carb weight loss has been used for about 150 years, and it is more effective than other diets

- Why does it work and how can the effects be maximized?

- It is not a coincidence that staying away from carbohydrates like bread and sugar has special benefits beyond the calories. Carbs cause your body to release insulin. Insulin is the body's fat-storing hormone.

- To be able to lose excess body fat, your first goal is reducing insulin levels. You do this by eating fewer carbs. For a lot of people, this will help them reach their weight loss goals.

- Weight loss is simply thought of as just calories – eat fewer calories, burn more calories, and you will lose weight. While this is true in theory, it is not useful practically as shown by an obesity epidemic during the time when people believed this.

- The main problem with just focusing on calories is it ignores hunger. It ignores the body's regulation of the fat is has stored. It ignores that if we don't eat calories, we eat food. Food is much more than just calories. Low carb foods will make you feel full. Other foods like soda will make you feel even more hungry.

- The idea of low carbs is to work with the body, not against it. Don't waste time and willpower on restricting calories, enduring hunger, and exercising - we need to do something else. We make our bodies want to eat less, and it will burn more of any excess we have.

- It does this by altering our hormonal balance. One hormone is most instrumental in doing this, and that is the fat-storing hormone insulin.

- Lowering insulin will increase fat burning, and this enables the body to release stored up body fat. This will result in less hunger and increased energy without exercising.

-

-

- STOCKING YOUR PANTRY

- Want to know what you can eat? What to stay away from? What can you indulge in now and then? Stock up on essentials and never buy what you don't need.

- When you start eating low-carb whole foods, there will be less food in your pantry since you will be buying less processed foods. You will be shopping the outer perimeters of the store for fresh fruits and vegetables, fish and meat, cheese and milk. Stay away from the inner aisles that hold all the processed foods.

- You might be wondering if it will cost more to eat low carb, but it is cheaper. You won't be buying chocolate, sweet treats, sugar, flour, rolls, wraps, bread, and junk food. Utilize the store's specials to find fruits and vegetables on sale. You might also find specials on meats.

- You will spend more money on good quality ingredients, but you will be shopping less. Anything you spend is an investment in your family and their health.

- You will also be saving money on taking out foods. One night's take out meal could easily add up to the same as feeding a family for a few days on healthy food.

- Check labels for fat and carb content as different brands can vary. Read every label on all the products you buy. It can be an eye-opener. You will learn what brands that are safe to buy and what to stay away from. Tuna might be packed with wheat and sugar; others are packed in olive oil.

- Healthy foods can have sugars added to them. When figuring out recipes, make sure you have picked the correct brand of food that you are using since nutritional values could vary. To figure out net carbs just subtract the fiber from the total carb value.

- Below you will find a shopping list:

• Sauces and Flavorings

- Full-fat mayonnaise

- Vinegars

- Fresh herbs

- Spices and herbs

- Himalayan salt

• Pantry Ingredients

- Almond meal and flour

- Sugar-free jelly

- Coconut shredded, unsweetened

- Cocoa

- Stevia, erythritol

- Coconut flour

- Ground almonds

- Nuts and seeds – stay away from cashews and peanuts

- Canned tomatoes

- Olives, stuffed or black

- ## **Fats and Oils**

- Stay away from seed oils like omega 6, canola, sunflower

- Macadamia oil

- Coconut oil

- Butter

- Olive oil

- Avocado oil

- ## **Dairy**

- Sour cream

- Haloumi

- Feta

- Full fat cream cheese

- Cream

- Full fat yogurt

- All types of cheeses

• **Fridge**

- Eggs – you can eat these any way you like – scrambled, omelet, fried, boiled, etc.

- Fish – sardines, tuna, hoki, mussels, shrimp - fresh and frozen, snapper, salmon, all fatty omega-3 rich seafood. Stay away from crumbled or battered fish.

- Lean meats

- Sausages – check labels to make sure it has high meat content without fillers.

- Chicken

- Bacon – no honey cured, or sugar added

- Free range or grass fed meats

- Ingredients for salads

- Fruits

- Vegetables except for root vegetables like potatoes, parsnips, carrots, etc.

- BREAKFAST

- BUNLESS BACON, EGG, AND CHEESE

- Serves: 1

- Ingredients:

- ¼ c shredded cheese

- 2 slices bacon, cooked

- ½ avocado, mashed

- 2 tbsp water

- 2 eggs

- Instructions:

- Place two Mason jar rings in a skillet. Spray everything with nonstick spray. Crack an egg into each of the lids and break up the yoke with a fork

- Pour the water into the skillet and place the lid on the skillet. Let the eggs steam for three minutes. Place cheese on one of the eggs, let cook until cheese melts.

- Place the egg, without the cheese, onto a plate. Add bacon and avocado. Place cheesy egg, cheese-side-down on top.

-

-
- EGGS WITH TOMATOES AND SCALLIONS

- Serves: 2

- Ingredients:

- Pepper and salt

- 1 tsp olive oil

- 1 large tomato, diced

- 4 scallions, diced

- 3 egg whites

- 2 eggs

- Instructions:

- Place oil in a skillet and heat. Mix in the tomatoes and scallions. Beat the eggs, pepper, and salt together. Pour the eggs into the skillet and scramble until done.

-

-
- BROCCOLI AND CHEESE OMELET

- Serves: 1

- Ingredients:

- Slice Swiss cheese

- ½ c broccoli, cooked

- Nonstick spray

- Pepper and salt

- 1 tbsp skim milk

- 2 egg whites

- 1 egg

- Instructions:

- Beat together pepper, salt, milk, and eggs. Heat a pan and spray with nonstick spray. Once warm, pour in the eggs a rotate to cover the bottom. Lower heat.

- Place the cheese down the center a top with broccoli. Once the egg is cooked, flip the edges over the fillings.

-
- FETA AND SPINACH FRITTATA

- Serves: 4

- Ingredients:

- Pepper and salt

- 2 tbsp grated Parmigiano-Reggiano

- 2-oz feta crumbled

- 10-oz thawed frozen spinach

- 3 chopped scallions

- ½ red onion, chopped

- 1 tsp olive oil

- 8 egg whites

- 2 eggs

- Instructions:

- Remove all water from the spinach.

- Heat the oil in a non-stick skillet.

- Place in the scallions and onion and cook four minutes, or until soft.

- Beat the eggs together and mix in spinach, cheeses, pepper, and salt.

- Pour into the hot skillet and let it cook for about five minutes, or until the bottom is set.

- Flip your frittata over in a manner that is most comfortable to you, and allow the other side to cook through.

- POACHED EGGS WITH ASPARAGUS

- Serves: 4

- Ingredients:

- 2 tbsp Parmigiano Reggiano

- Pepper and salt

- 4 eggs

- 2 bunches asparagus, ends removed

- Instructions:

- Steam the asparagus until they are tender-crisp, and then run under cool water to stop the cooking. Drain and place onto four different plates.

- Poach each egg. Take them out with a slotted spoon and place an egg on top of each asparagus bunch. Top with the cheese, pepper, and salt.

-

-

- EGG-IN-A-HOLE

- Serves: 4

- Ingredients:

- Pepper and salt

- 4 eggs

- 1 bell pepper, sliced in 4 ½ in rings

- Nonstick spray

- Instructions:

- Heat up a skillet and spray with nonstick spray. Place in the pepper and allow it to cook for a minute. Crack an egg into each pepper ring and season with pepper and salt. Allow to cook until the eggs are done to your liking. Two to three minutes will bring the eggs to runny.

-

-
- BAKED EGGS IN SPINACH

- Serves: 4

- Ingredients:

- Nonstick spray

- 2 tbsp asiago cheese

- Pepper and salt

- 4 eggs

- 1 ½ lb baby spinach

- ¼ c shallots, diced

- 2 tsp olive oil

- Instructions:

- Your oven should be set to 400. Spray four small oven-safe dishes with nonstick spray.

- Add oil to a pan and heat. Add in the shallots and cook for two to three minutes. Mix in the pepper, salt, and spinach, cooking until wilted. Stir in the asiago.

- Divide the spinach between the dishes and form and well in the center. Crack an egg into each and top with pepper and salt. Place the dishes on baking sheets and cook about 17 minutes or until the yolks are set to your liking.

-

-

- MAIN DISHES

- CHICKEN FAJITA BOWLS

- Serves: 4

- Ingredients:

- 2 tbsp lime juice

- 2 tsp cumin

- 24-oz bag riced cauliflower

- 1 tsp salt

- 1 tsp garlic powder

- 1/3 c cilantro, chopped

- 2 tsp paprika

- 2 tbsp EVOO

- 1 sweet onion, sliced

- 3 bell peppers, sliced

- 2 tsp chili powder

- 1 lb chicken breasts, boneless skinless

- Instructions:

- Your oven should be at 400. Put the chicken on half of a baking sheet and the onions and peppers on the other. Drizzle everything with olive oil.

- Mix the salt, garlic, cumin, paprika, and chili powder together. Sprinkle over the veggies and chicken. Make sure that you toss the veggies and flip the chicken so that everything is coated. Bake for 20 minutes.

- Meanwhile, cook the cauliflower as the bag says to. After finished, toss with lime juice and cilantro. Serve everything together and top with avocado, sour cream, or cheese.

-

-
- STEAK TACO SALAD

- Serves: 4

- Ingredients:

- 2 sliced green onions

- 1 tsp oregano

- 1 c halved cherry tomatoes

- 1 c black beans, drained and rinsed

- 1 romaine head, chopped

- Salt

- 1 c corn

- 1 tsp cumin

- 2 limes, juiced

- 1 tbsp taco seasoning

- ¾ lb steak

- ¼ c + 1 tbsp EVOO, divided

- Instructions:

- Heat a tablespoon of oil in a pan. Coat the steak with the taco seasoning. Cook until it is cooked to your liking, flip only once. Place on a cutting board and allow to rest for five minutes; slice against the grain.

- As the steak cooks, make the dressing. Whisk the oregano, cumin, lime juice, and the rest of the oil together, and then season with salt.

- In a large bowl, add in the onion, tomatoes, beans, corn, steak, and romaine. Season with salt and top with dressing.

-

-

- MUSSELS IN BASIL SAUCE

- Serves: 3

- Ingredients:

- Pepper and salt

- ¼ c parmesan

- 2 tbsp olive oil

- ½ c basil

- ½ c half and half, fat-free

- ½ c white wine

- 2 garlic cloves

- 1 garlic clove, smashed a chopped

- 1 shallot, minced

- 2 tsp butter

- Instructions:

- De-bread and scrub your mussels in cold water. Get rid of any cracked shells. Using a large pot, melt the butter. Place in the chopped garlic and shallots and sauté for about three minutes. Pour in the wine and allow to boil. Place in the mussels and top with the lid Allow cooking four to six minutes until the mussels open. Once cooked, remove from the pot with a slotted spoon. Get rid of any that didn't open.

- Add ¼ of a cup of half and half to the pot and let simmer for four minutes.

- Place the rest of the garlic, half and half, olive oil, parmesan, and basil in a blender and puree. Pour into the pot and add pepper and salt. Let simmer a few minutes long then serve over top of the mussels.

-

-

- GARLIC LEMON TILAPIA

- Serves: 6

- Ingredients:

- Nonstick spray

- 2 tbsp butter

- Pepper and salt

- 4 tsp parsley

- 2 tbsp lemon juice

- 4 crushed garlic cloves

- 6 6-oz tilapia filets

- Instructions:

- Your oven should be set to 400.

- Melt the butter in a small skillet. Cook the garlic for a minute. Mix in the lemon juice and turn off the heat.

- Coat a casserole dish with nonstick spray.

- Put the fish in the dish and season with pepper and salt. Pour the butter mixture over the fish and then sprinkle with the parsley.

- Cook for about 15 minutes.

-
- CHICKEN WITH ARTICHOKE AND FETA

- Serves: 6

- Ingredients:

- Pepper and salt

- 2 tbsp parsley, chopped

- ¼ c feta cheese, reduced-fat

- 1 tsp oregano

- 1 crushed garlic clove

- 6-oz jar artichoke hearts

- 6 chicken thighs, boneless and skinless

- Instructions:

- Place the artichoke hearts, and their juice, in a bag with the chicken. Allow them to marinate at least 20 minutes. Drain the liquid and mix in the pepper, salt, oregano, and garlic.

- Broil the chicken for about ten minutes. Flip the chicken and cook another eight to ten minutes, or until fully cooked. Top with the feta and cook long enough to melt. Serve with fresh parsley.

-
- PORK CHOPS WITH MUSHROOMS

- Serves: 4

- Ingredients:

- 2 tbsp parsley, chopped

- 1 tbsp Dijon

- 10-oz baby Bella mushrooms, sliced

- 1 c chicken stock, low-sodium

- ¼ c shallots, chopped

- Pepper

- ½ tsp salt

- 4 pork chops, bone-in

- 1 tsp ghee

- Instructions:

- Melt the ghee in a large skillet. Top with pepper and salt on both sides of all the pork chops. Sauté the chops in the skillet for seven minutes, flip, and cook for another seven minutes. The thermometer should red 160F. Remove the pork and keep warm.

- Place the shallots in the pan and cook for about three minutes. Pour in the stock and deglaze the pan. Mix in the pepper, mushrooms, one tablespoon parsley, and mustard. Cook for about three minutes. Serve the chops topped with the gravy and sprinkle with the remaining parsley.

-

- THAI CURRY SHRIMP

- Serves: 4

- Ingredients:

- Salt

- 2 tbsp basil, chopped

- 2 tsp Thai fish sauce

- 6-oz coconut milk

- 1 lb shrimp, cleaned

- 2 minced garlic cloves

- 1 tbsp Thai green curry paste

- 4 scallions, chopped

- 1 tsp oil

- Instructions:

- Heat oil in a large skillet. Place in the white parts of the scallion and curry paste. Cook for a minute.

- Mix in the salt, garlic, and shrimp. Cook for another two to three minutes.

- Pour in the fish sauce and coconut milk. Simmer for two to three minutes, or until the shrimp is fully cooked.

- Take it off the heat and mix in the basil and scallion greens. Serve with basmati rice.

-

- SIDES AND SNACKS

- LOADED CAULIFLOWER BITES

- Serves: 6

- Ingredients:

- 1 tbsp chives, chopped

- 5 bacon slices, cooked and crumbled

- 1 c shredded cheese

- 1 tsp garlic powder

- Pepper

- Salt

- 2 tbsp EVOO

- 1 head cauliflower, cut into florets

- Cooking spray

- Instructions:

- Your oven should be at 425. Spray a baking sheet with nonstick spray.

- Bring salted water to a boil and cook the cauliflower for about five minutes, and then drain.

- Spread them on the baking sheet and coat with the garlic, pepper, salt, and oil. With a potato masher or glass, smash the florets.

- Top each smash with some bacon, and cheese. Bake for about 15 minutes. Sprinkle them with chives.

- HASSELBACK ZUCCHINI

- Serves: 4

- Ingredients:

- ¼ tsp red pepper flakes

- Salt

- ¼ c parmesan

- 3 tbsp EVOO

- 1 lb zucchini, ends cut off

- Instructions:

- Your oven should be at 400. Cut slices into the zucchini making sure not to cut all the way through. Using two wooden spoons as guides can help.

- Drizzle with the oil and season with the red pepper flakes, salt, and parmesan.

- Cook for about 25 minutes. It should be golden and tender.

-

- DEVILED EGGS

- Serves: 4

- Ingredients:

- 2 tbsp chives, chopped

- Pepper and salt

- Paprika

- 1 tsp Dijon

- 2 tbsp light mayo

- 4 hard boiled eggs, cooled and peeled

- Instructions:

- Slice the eggs long-ways. Remove the yolks and place them in a small bowl. Mix in the pepper, salt, mustard, and mayo. Mix well and place them in a piping bad. Pipe the mixture into the egg white and top with paprika and chives.

-

-

- AUTUMN SALAD WITH GORGONZOLA AND PEARS

- Serves: 6

- Ingredients:

- Dressing:

- 3 tbsp olive oil

- Pepper

- ¼ tsp salt

- 1 tsp honey

- ½ tsp Dijon

- 2 tbsp red wine vinegar

- Salad:

- 1-oz pecans

- 8-oz mixed baby greens

- ¼ c gorgonzola cheese, crumbled

- 2 small ripe pears, diced and peeled

- Instructions:

- Mix the pepper, salt, honey, mustard, and vinegar together. Whisk in the oil until it all comes together.

- Combine all of the salad ingredients together. Once you are ready to serve, top with the vinaigrette and toss.

- ROASTED BROCCOLI WITH GARLIC

- Serves: 4

- Ingredients:

- Pepper and salt

- 2 tbsp EVOO

- 6 smashed garlic cloves

- 1 ½ lb broccoli florets

- Instructions:

- Your oven should be set at 450. In your baking dish, mix the pepper, salt, garlic, olive oil, and broccoli. Cook for about 20 minutes. The broccoli should be tender and brown.

-

-

- SPAGHETTI SQUASH PESTO

- Serves: 4

- Ingredients:

- 1 tomato, diced

- Pepper and salt

- 3 tbsp Parmigiano-Reggiano

- ¼ c olive oil

- 1 small garlic clove

- 15 basil leaves

- 1 small spaghetti squash

- Instructions:

- Slice the squash in half and scoop out seeds and fibers. Place the squash in a microwaveable dish and cover. Microwave for eight to nine minutes. Take out of the microwave and scoop out the flesh with a fork, and place in a large bowl.

- In a blender, mix the pepper, salt, cheese, olive oil, garlic, and basil until smooth.

- Mix two cups spaghetti squash with the pesto and toss in the pepper, salt, and tomatoes.

-
- PUMPKIN SEEDS

- Serves: varies

- Ingredients:

- Salt

- Olive oil spray

- Pumpkin seeds

- Instructions:

- Clean the pumpkin seeds.

- Spread the seeds on a baking sheet and let it dry overnight.

- Your oven should be set to 250. Lightly coat the seeds with cooking spray or oil and sprinkle with as much salt as you like

- Cook them until they turn golden. This should take about an hour and fifteen minutes.

- Allow to cool and enjoy.

-

-

-

- DESSERTS
-

- OVEN-BAKED BRIE CHEESE

- Serves: 4

- Ingredients:

- 1 tbsp olive oil

- Pepper and salt

- 1 tbsp rosemary

- 1 garlic clove

- 2-oz pecan

- 8 ¾-oz Brie

- Instructions:

- Your oven should be at 400. Place parchment paper on a baking sheet and lay the cheese on top.

- Chop the herbs and nuts and mince the garlic. Mix them together with the olive oil and season with pepper and salt. Place the mixture on the cheese and cook for ten minutes.

-

-
- PINEAPPLE ZUCCHINI CAKE

- Serves: 16

- Ingredients:

- Cake:

- 20-oz crushed pineapple, drained

- 2 c zucchini, grated

- 1 tsp vanilla

- 2 eggs

- 3 tbsp canola oil

- 1 tsp salt

- Pinch ginger

- ¼ tsp nutmeg

- 2 tsp cinnamon

- 2 tsp baking soda

- 1 c sugar

- ¾ c whole wheat flour

- ¾ c AP flour

- ½ c coconut, flaked

- Frosting:

- 1 tsp vanilla

- 1 c powdered sugar

- 8-oz 1/3 fat cream cheese

- Instructions:

- Your oven should be set to 350. Mix the spices, salt, baking soda, coconut, sugar, and flours.

- Mix the vanilla, eggs, and oil together. Stir in the pineapple and zucchini. Fold the wet into the dry ingredients. It will start out dry and stiff but continue to mix; it will eventually come together.

- Coat a Bundt pan with cooking spray and spoon in the batter. Bake for 33 to 40 minutes. Let the cake cool on wire rack completely before frosting.

- For the frosting: beat all of the frosting ingredients together. Spread the frosting on the cake and top with chopped pecans if you want.

-
- CINNAMON APPLES WITH VANILLA SAUCE

- Serves: 6

- Ingredients:

- Sauce:

- 2 c heavy cream

- 1 egg yolk

- 2 tbsp butter

- 1 star anise

- ½ tsp vanilla

- 8 tbsp heavy cream

- Apples:

- 1 tsp cinnamon

- 3 apples, preferably tart and firm

- 3 tbsp butter

- Instructions:

- Bring the eight tablespoons of heavy cream, star anise, vanilla, and butter to a boil. Turn the heat down and allow to simmer for five minutes. It should turn creamy.

- Take it off the heat and take out the star anise. Mix in the yolk and whisk vigorously. Allow the mixture to cool completely

- Whisk the 2 cups of heavy cream with the completely cold cream mix.

- Let the mixture refrigerate for 30 minutes.

- Wash, core, and slice the apples. Melt the butter in a skillet and brown up the apple slices. Mix in the cinnamon until almost done.

- Serve the apples topped with the vanilla sauce.

-

-

- CRUNCHY BERRY MOUSSE

- Serves: 8

- Ingredients:

- ¼ tsp vanilla

- ½ lemon, zested

- 1 ¾ oz chopped pecans

- 3 ¼ oz mixed berries

- 2 c heavy cream

- Instructions:

- Place the cream in a bowl and whip until soft peaks begin to form. Mix in the vanilla and lemon zest.

- Gently fold in the nuts and berries.

- Top the bowl with cling wrap and refrigerate the mixture for at least three hours, or until the mixture has firmed into a mousse. If you don't mind a less firm consistency, then you can enjoy it immediately.

-

-
- LOW-CARB CHOCOLATE MOUSSE

- Serves: 6

- Ingredients:

- 3 1/3 c coconut milk

- 2 to 3 tbsp. cocoa powder

- 1 tsp. vanilla extract

- 1 tsp. honey

- Instructions:

- Put coconut milk in the fridge for four hours until the cream separates from the water.

- Open can carefully and spoon out the cream and place in a bowl. Keep the coconut water for pancakes or smoothies.

- Whisk the cream, vanilla, and honey with a hand mixer until thick. Add cocoa and whisk more.

- Serve in dessert bowls.

- If you place the mousse in the freezer for about an hour, you will have ice cream.

- SALTY CHOCOLATE TREAT

- Serves: 10

- Ingredients:

- 3 ½ oz. dark chocolate, minimum of 70 % cocoa

- 10 hazelnuts, walnuts, or pecans

- 2 tbsp. roasted unsweet coconut chips

- 1 tbsp. pumpkin seeds

- Sea salt

- Instructions:

- Melt chocolate. Have 10 small cupcake liner. No bigger than 2 inches.

- Put melted chocolate into the liners.

- Add seeds, coconut chips, and nuts. Sprinkle with salt.

- Allow to cool and store in the fridge.

- If you don't have cupcake liners, you can pour the chocolate into a small dish lined with parchment paper about 8 x 8 inches. Place coconut, nuts, and sea salt onto chocolate before it is completely hard. Once completely hardened, break up into pieces. You could add chili for flavor or some dry berries such as goji or blueberries if you are not sensitive to sugar.

- CREAMY COTTAGE CHEESE PUDDING

- Serves: 6

- Ingredients:

- 2/3 lbs. cottage cheese

- 1 ¼ c heavy whipping cream

- 1 tsp vanilla extract

- 1 tsp ground cinnamon

- 2 oz. fresh raspberries or berry of choice

- Instructions:

- Whip heavy cream until it forms soft peaks. Add vanilla. Mix in cinnamon or sprinkle on top before serving.

- Gently fold in cottage cheese. Do not over mix. Let pudding sit in fridge about 10 to 15 minutes.

- Serve with red berries of choice either mashed or whole. Wedges of oranges or Clementine are delicious as well.

-

-
- CONCLUSION
-

- Thank for making it through to the end of *The Ultimate Low Carb Cookbook.* Let's hope it was informative and able to provide you with all of the tools you need to achieve your goals.

- Now you have plenty of recipes to get you

started on your weight loss journey. You have all the information you need, and the recipes to get you started, so start today.

-
-
-
-
-
-
-
-
-
-
-

-
-
-
-
-